DAVID MUENCH

Cliff Palace, Mesa Verde National Park

. . . in this land of room enough and time enough.

Great White Throne, Zion National Park

GRAND CIRCLE ADVENTURE

Like a fabulous jewel encircled by incredibly beautiful gems, Lake Powell in Utah and Arizona is set amidst an enchanting ring of natural spectacles: national parks and monuments with rugged mountains thrusting to lofty heights, deep canyons, high cliffs, and fantastic arches, plus a host of nostalgic old villages, ghost towns, and prehistoric Indian ruins—all inviting exploration.

This region is an unparalleled vacationland. Today, thanks to planning with an eye for scenic adventure and an all-weather highway system, you can see it all with comfort and convenience in one complete circuit. It is called the "Grand Circle Adventure." And grand it is—a 900-mile loop around some of the most spectacular country on earth.

Within the circle are seven national parks: Bryce Canyon, Zion, Capitol Reef, Arches, Canyonlands, the Grand Canyon, and Mesa Verde, plus seven national monuments: Navajo, Natural Bridges, Cedar Breaks, Pipe Spring, Canyon de Chelly, Hovenweep, and Rainbow Bridge. There are also state parks, historical sites, Monument Valley Navajo Tribal Park, and Glen Canyon National Recreation Area.

by Allen C. Reed

Book design by K. C. DenDooven, Edited by Mary Lu Moore

Front cover: Grand Canyon by Ed Cooper, Mesa Verde by David Muench, Monument Valley by Ed Cooper, Rainbow Bridge by Ed Cooper.
Page 4: Monument Valley by Josef Muench. Title page: Turret Arch by David Muench. Pages 6/7: Lake Powell by John Lahusen.
Back cover: Rainbow Bridge by David Muench.

Second Printing, 1987

FROM THE NEWEST (around 53 million years old) "icing" on the geological layer cake at Bryce Canyon and Cedar Breaks to some of the oldest exposed rock on earth at the bottom of the Grand Canyon, our circle tour touches four different biogeographic zones. The span of these life zones reaches from the upper pine, spruce, and aspen forests of Bryce, Kaibab, Cedar Mountain, Boulder Mountain, and Mesa Verde down to the canyon-bottom Sonoran zone as found in southern Arizona and northwestern Mexico. With some overlapping, each zone supports its own variety of plant and animal life. Some of these higher zones, thrust up along the perimeter of the circuit, are always in sight, beckoning the traveler to enjoy an alpine side trip into a mountainous national forest.

The Grand Circle Adventure can start and end at any point of choice. The most practical approach is to start at the place most convenient for you, then set your own pace and enjoy.

GLEN CANYON DAM, PAGE, AND WAHWEAP AREA OF LAKE POWELL

At the center of our Grand Circle Adventure is the 1,869-square-mile Glen Canyon National Recreation Area with its centerpiece: beautiful Lake Powell. This second largest man-made lake on earth is 190 miles long. Its meandering 1,960-mile canyon-serrated shoreline is longer than the entire coastline of California.

A good place to start your tour is right at the water's edge in Arizona, at Wahweap Lodge and Marina. Art Greene founded this recreational area and developed it over a 22-year period. In addition to the modern lodge with its spectacular lake-view rooms, the glass-walled convention and dining room offers such a sweeping panorama of scenic splendor that the 600 people it will accommodate spend as much time staring as they do eating. You will find both a pool at the lodge and a wide sandy swimming beach at the lake, in addition to all the available water activities and wide choice of special water cruises available. Or you could try a variety of four-wheel-drive land tours, also offered at the lodge. A trailer, camper, and mobile-home village also overlooks the lake, and a large National Park Service campground is close by.

The key commercial center of this remote recreation area is the newer town of Page, on a mesa overlooking the dam. Whatever you may have forgotten to bring along can most likely be found in the many modern, well-stocked stores and supermarkets here. An hour or so spent in the John Wesley Powell Museum, operated by the Page Chamber of Commerce, is an ideal way to start informing yourself about what this section of Grand Circle Adventure country is all about.

STEVEN WARD

It's time for water fun at Lake Powell. Ski or boat on it; swim or scuba in it; para-sail above it; camp by it. Gear up for trout, bass, or numerous other species from a 1-pound bluegill to a 25-pound channel cat. Lake Powell, at the heart of Glen Canyon National Recreation Area, has it all.

Lake Powell, with its variety of things to do and its majestic scenic surroundings in all their dramatic moods, can be the perfect panacea for pent-up pressures. Even without a boat, the Glen Canyon National Recreation Area offers visitors and hikers an invitation to enjoy a tranquil rendezvous with the soul.

GARY LADD

Gregory Butte no doubt blended in with scores of kindred desert promontories in 1776 when Spanish missionary-explorers Escalante and Domínguez crossed the Colorado River three miles west at present Padre Bay. Today, like a stately, isolated castle, it soars high above its Lake Powell moat at Last Chance Bay, halfway between Wahweap and Rainbow Bridge.

ALLEN C. REED

Page can be the gateway to still more delightful adventures in the area, such as a memorable one-day float trip on the Colorado River between towering 2,000-foot canyon walls. The starting point is beneath Glen Canyon Bridge, one of the world's highest steel arch bridges (700 feet overhead), located next to Glen Canyon Dam. The float ends 15 miles downriver at historic Lee's Ferry.

The Glen Canyon Dam is an impressive sight. Both the exhibits at the Carl Hayden Visitor Center and a self-conducted tour through the immense power plant and inner workings of the dam are valuable experiences.

In 1963 Glen Canyon Dam was completed and became operational. The last generator was installed and dedicated in 1966, nearly ten years after the first construction began. The concrete arch rising 710 feet above bedrock holds back 27 million acre-feet of water at full-lake capacity. Inside, 600 feet down in an inner chamber, you will gaze upon a battery of eight immense whirring generating units spun by the escaping waters of Lake Powell. The maximum 1,124,000 kilowatts generated by this power plant, flowing to population centers like Las Vegas, Phoenix, Tucson, and smaller communities, is enough to supply continually a city of approximately one million residents.

One of man's mightiest engineering sculptures, Glen Canyon Dam was created to collect the waters from five rivers: the Colorado, San Juan, Dirty Devil, Escalante, and Green. The lake was named after the first of the pioneer Colorado River explorers, John Wesley Powell. Delightful glens, grand grottos, and majestic towering canyon walls inspired him to give Glen Canyon its name.

On any summer day you can see recreation participants taking full advantage of Lake Powell's offerings: sailing, fishing, water skiing, para-sailing, or swimming. On the lake every size of watercraft from inflatable neoprene vessels to 60-foot cruisers is represented; yet there is enough water space to offer a degree of privacy to them all. A common sight arriving or leaving the Wahweap Marina are houseboats loaded with vacationers making their home on the water for a while.

In the midst of all this action, you can also just meditate. You can enjoy the drama of ever-changing moods of light and shadow on the vast backdrop of magnificently carved monuments and canyon walls that thrust hundreds of feet above the lake while they plunge brilliant color reflections equally as deep into the dark water below.

The vast bays of Lake Powell offer plenty of uncrowded play space. Close to a hundred winding, isolated tributary canyons offer fascinating invitations to explore. Many narrow down until the walls brush both sides of even a small boat, leaving no choice but to back out in search of a wider place to turn around.

For the rod-and-reel enthusiast there is year-

A battery of eight immense turbine-driven generators hum to the tune of several thousand cubic feet of water per second surging through 15-foot-in-diameter penstocks from Lake Powell. The maximum Glen Canyon Dam electrical production capacity is enough to supply a city of a million people. All this can be seen and is explained on a self-guided tour that starts and ends at the dam's Carl Hayden Visitor and Exhibit Center.

round fishing for striped and largemouth bass, walleye, rainbow and brown trout, bluegill, sunfish, crappie, pike, and channel cat. Stripers up to 31.5 pounds and crappie up to 3 pounds have been taken from Lake Powell. Below the dam, where the cold deep lake water spills out through the penstocks and turbines into the Colorado River, it is not uncommon to pull in large trout. The current record is an 18.3-pound brown trout.

The Glen Canyon National Recreation Area cuts diagonally across the southeast corner of Utah. In just a few hours round trip, you can visit the Paria River canyon, vividly striped with as bright a spectrum of nature's geological coloring as can be found anywhere in the world. Or you can prowl through a weathered movie set where many scenes were filmed for such major motion pictures as *McKenna's Gold, Bandolero, Planet of the Apes, Outlaw Josie Wales,* and the *Superman* series.

In less than an hour by jeep from the lodge, you can walk in the quiet of the sandy floor of Sculpture Canyon. This wild exhibit of natural artistry, carved by centuries of periodic swirling flood waters, is a fantasy of sensational stone whirls and twists. The canyon is so narrow at the top that in some places you can step across it.

No visit to the area is complete without a cruise

For a brief moment the rising sun, from its crown-jewel crest on distant Navajo Mountain, silhouettes towering Gunsight Butte. Campers on sandy beaches, in quiet coves, in hidden canyons, or beside yawning bays are in perfect positions for a get-up-early preview of true Lake Powell serenity as the first rays of daybreak brush the sleeping buttes and shimmering lake into a watercolor masterpiece.

Quite likely there is no better way to close a perfect day than to be romanced by Lake Powell on a sunset champagne-dinner cruise on the Canyon King. From Wahweap Lodge this double-deck paddle-wheeler churns out on a most informative and relaxing excursion every summer evening.

Lake Powell Country

Lake Powell means different things to different people: water conservation, hydroelectric power, flood control, water recreation. The most notable attraction of all is the grand-scale recreational appeal of this immense aquatic playground in its captivating surroundings. This 186-mile jagged-edged splash of blue, in its astonishingly wild and rugged warm-toned country, prowls enough serpentine side canyons to acquire a shoreline well over 1,900 miles long. More than two million enthusiastic pleasure-seekers come to Glen Canyon National Recreation Area each year to play. A lot of watercraft can cruise a lake this size and not get in anyone's way.

Five lakeside recreation headquarters and marinas owned and operated by the Del Webb Corporation are located roughly 50 miles apart. The modern, luxurious Wahweap Lodge and Marina, near Glen Canyon Dam, is the largest facility. Bullfrog Resort and Marina and Halls Crossing and Hite marinas, complete with boat rentals, services, and supplies, are all reached by excellent paved highways. The fifth marina, Dangling Rope, is accessible only by boat.

Everything that swims or floats seems to be present on the lake—from scuba divers to large cruisers and tour boats. All summer long, perky white sails perform graceful watercolor ballets. Powerboats zip across wide bays, towing

All four resort marinas rent houseboats. Families, clubs, and groups of friends have discovered the Lake Powell–houseboat combination as the perfect luxury vacation getaway.

Tour boats leave Wahweap daily to explore a variety of scenic adventures. The favorite excursion is that of docking in the inspiring presence of magnificent Rainbow Bridge.

Wahweap Lodge and Marina has fast become one of America's grandest lakeside resorts. Over two million visitors a year— from one or two vacationers up to full-fledged conventions—agree. Lodging, dining, cocktail lounge, shops, swimming pool, beach, campground, boat tours, rentals, supplies, launching, and other services make Wahweap the ideal gateway to the water wonderland of Lake Powell.

either exhilarated water skiers or those more adventuresome, dangling from high-flying para-sails. A one-hundred-foot-long paddle-wheeler, *The Canyon King*, offers delightful sunset champagne-and-dinner cruises from Wahweap Lodge. Lake Powell is also "houseboat heaven." Some boaters bring their own home-away-from-home; others rent. They can cruise for days, seldom seeing the same scenery twice.

For the rod-and-reeler, extraordinary year-round fishing yields largemouth and striped bass (record: 31.5 pounds), rainbow and brown trout (record: 17 pounds), crappie, bluegill, walleye, sunfish, pike, and channel cat.

Lake Powell is truly "Paradise Found." The many moods of buttes, towers, arches, coves, grottos, plunging reflections, mysterious side canyons, wildlife, and all the rest can put a real strain on your camera. As you sit by a fragrant driftwood campfire on an isolated sandy beach, a snug tent pitched behind you, the soft splashing waves of the lake caressing your tied-down boat, the stars and moon glinting in the ripples bless you with an "all's well" feeling that is pretty hard to beat.

There is a lot of history around here, too, like the "Crossing of the Fathers." Spanish missionary explorers forded the Colorado River over 200 years ago, searching for a direct route between Santa Fe, New Mexico, and Monterey, California. You can take your boat within 500 feet of the site in Padre Bay . . . only that 500 feet is straight down!

The lake is named in honor of Major John Wesley Powell. He passed this way, 500 feet down, too. But that was well over a hundred years ago. Major Powell, a Civil War veteran, had lost one arm in the battle of Shiloh, but that did not stop him from being the first explorer through the treacherous Colorado River canyons—all the way.

The crowning glory of a visit to Lake Powell country is the imposing magnificence of Rainbow Bridge. You can get within a few steps of it in your own boat, by charter boat, or on a regularly scheduled tour. To the Navajo, this "rainbow turned to stone" is most sacred. It may well impress you that way too, as you stand silently in its presence. Its sheer elegance penetrates to the very depths of your soul.

If the scores of complimentary adjectives published over the years to describe the Rainbow Bridge and Lake Powell country were laid end to end, there is little doubt that they would reach all the way to the absolute truth.

For reservations and information contact:
Del E. Webb Recreational Properties, P. O. Box 29040, Phoenix, Arizona 85038, 1-800-528-6154, 1-602-278-8888 (in Arizona), TELEX 16-5092.

up lake to the most sensational naturally sculptured feature of them all, the world's highest known stone arch: the graceful 290-foot-high Rainbow Bridge. Before Lake Powell backed up into Forbidding Canyon, Rainbow Bridge was inaccessible to all but a few hardy hikers. Today this fabulous sight is just a few steps from a courtesy boat dock.

You can make the 48-mile trip from Wahweap Marina to Rainbow Bridge in your own boat, a rental boat, a chartered boat with guide, or on one of the many regular tour boats. However you go, Rainbow Bridge National Monument is an absolute must.

NAVAJO NATIONAL MONUMENT

The next leg of your circuitous journey will be on Arizona State Highway 98, eastward across a section of the Navajo Reservation and past the tall stacks of the Navajo Power Generating Station. In the distance, that large blue-gray mound that seems to follow right along with you is 10,380-foot Navajo Mountain, a symbol sacred to the Navajo.

About 52 miles southeast of Page, a side road to the north is marked "Inscription House Ruin." This ancient Indian cliff dwelling of 74 units was constructed sometime around A.D. 1274. It is part of the Navajo National Monument, but it is now closed indefinitely because of urgent stabilization needs. After reaching U.S. Highway 160, just 12 miles farther on, you travel another 13 miles north on 160 to intersecting Arizona Highway 564. It is then just nine miles on 564 to the visitor center of Navajo National Monument.

Here a trail leads to an overlook above Betatakin (Beh-TAH-tah-kin), second of the three major ruins in the monument. The hike takes less than one hour round trip. This 135-room cliff dwelling is nestled in a 500-foot-high cave in the canyon wall opposite you. If you want a more intimate look, scheduled ranger-conducted hikes will take you there. But be prepared for a three-hour round trip. Descending the 700 feet to the canyon floor is no problem; just so you remember that it will be uphill all the way back, at a breath-shortening altitude of over 7,000 feet.

The largest cliff dwelling in Arizona, Keet Seel, also is located in Navajo National Monument. Here there are 160 rooms and six ceremonial chambers called *kivas* (KEE-vahs). It is a full day round trip to Keet Seel. To visit this cliff dwelling you must register at park headquarters at least a day in advance. Visitation is limited to 15 persons a day, April through September. The primitive eight-mile trail to the ruin crosses the canyon stream numerous times. If all the arduous hiking with wet feet doesn't really appeal to you, horses and Navajo guides are available.

CANYON DE CHELLY

Returning to U.S. 160, turn northeast and proceed 19 miles to the Kayenta junction, then go 8

Most Navajo children grow up around sheep, for herding—as well as shearing, carding, spinning, dyeing, and weaving of wool into rugs—has long been an important part of everyday Navajo life.

miles beyond it to Navajo Highway 59. Take Navajo 59 southeast 54 miles to U.S. 191 (formerly Arizona 63) at Many Farms. From there it is 13 miles farther south to the Chinle turnoff and the mouth of Canyon de Chelly National Monument.

At Thunderbird Lodge near the park headquarters, the highway splits, offering two splendid scenic rim drives. Navajo Highway 7, following the old Fort Defiance Trail on the south side of the canyon, leads to sensational overlooks from 500 to 1,000 feet above the floor of Canyon de Chelly, including the spectacular White House cliff dwelling and Spider Rock.

Navajo Highway 64 along the north rim leads to great views of Canyon del Muerto in the Canyon de Chelly monument and of ruins including a photographer's favorite: Antelope House cliff dwelling.

In this enchanting setting Thunderbird Lodge, offering excellent rooms, dining, and canyon tours, is open all year. A park service campground with no hookups is located nearby.

To get to the next stop on the Grand Circle Adventure, you can backtrack to Kayenta junction,

Arches, monuments, and small ruins are isolated on the top or in the candy-striped canyons of White Mesa just south of Arizona State Highway 98 between Page and U.S. 160.

In Navajo National Monument three of Arizona's largest cliff dwellings: Inscription House, Betatakin, and Keet Seel, were once home for several hundred prehistoric Indians known as the Anasazi. Along with other ancient southwest dwellings, these were suddenly deserted around the close of the thirteenth century.

A spectacular overlook of the 135-room Betatakin ruin 700 feet below is located near the visitor center and museum at Navajo National Monument. For enthusiasts of hiking, close-up photography, or Indian lore, regular ranger-guided descents offer access to the canyon floor.

DAVID MUENCH

then travel 24 miles north on U.S. 163 to the Utah border and Monument Valley.

MONUMENT VALLEY NAVAJO TRIBAL PARK

Monument Valley tour information is available, and modern accommodations are open the year around at Kayenta and at Mexican Hat, Utah, 21 miles northeast. The closest room, meal, and tour accommodations are in Monument Valley one mile west of U.S. 163 at Goulding's Lodge and Trading Post on the Utah–Arizona border, right at the Valley door. A trailer and tent campground also is located there, and another is situated next to the visitor center three miles east of U.S. 163.

Travel into the Valley by private car is confined to limited sections of dirt roads. To enjoy the innermost reaches where you can experience the Valley at its best, to visit the Navajo at home—an octagonal dwelling called a *hogan* (ho-GAHN), and to learn what it is you are seeing and where you are at all times, your best bet is a four-wheel-drive tour. The licensed, well-informed guide is usually a Navajo who grew up in the area and who knows every arch, monument, and Navajo in the Valley.

This mile-high monument-studded western scenic paradise is completely within the land of the Navajo. For the most part these gentle and hospitable people still lead a pastoral life as dry farmers and sheepmen. Their traditional cedar-log and mud-plastered hogans blend perfectly into the 1,500 square miles that make up Monument Valley.

Among Navajo women velveteen blouses in vivid blues, greens, yellows, purples, and reds and decorated with silver coins are still worn with equally colorful satiny ankle-length skirts. Treasures of handmade silver and turquoise jewelry adorn both Navajo men and women. The Navajo are well known as silversmiths and rug weavers.

In the inevitable, ever-changing pattern of progress, some of the traditional Navajo hogans throughout the Valley have given way to small, conventional block-and-frame dwellings. The familiar old horse-drawn spring wagons, filled with picturesque Navajo families, and creeping along sandy ruts, have in many cases been replaced by pickup trucks, churning up cockscombs of dust on reservation roads or zipping along the now hard-surfaced highways to Kayenta or Flagstaff.

Monument Valley is truly an artistic creation of nature, with its stately, photogenic carved red sandstone buttes and slender monoliths jutting into the sky and bearing names like "The Totem Pole," "The Three Sisters," "Rooster Rock," and "Pioneer Woman." Then there are the numerous wind- and weather-carved arches with descriptive names such as "The Sun's Eye," "Moccasin Arch," "Ear of the Wind," "The Great Hogan," and "Spider Web Arch."

The arches, monuments, and sand dunes of Monument Valley have made spectacular backdrops for scores of motion pictures ever since 1938. In

Canyon de Chelly's Spider Rock rises higher than an 80-story building, yet it could scarcely accommodate a one-room office on top. Legend makes this the home of Spider Woman, who carries small Navajo children to the top and eats them if they are not well behaved.

that year trading post operator Harry Goulding introduced the Valley to John Ford who then brought in John Wayne to star in *Stagecoach*. More major productions directed by Ford followed: *She Wore a Yellow Ribbon, Fort Apache, Cheyenne Autumn,* and *The Searchers*. Hardly a season has gone by over the last 40 years without a movie or television commercial of some sort being filmed among the monuments.

Though the monuments we see have been slowly weathering away for millions of years since they were part of a vast upthrust ocean bed plateau, the change witnessed in a lifetime is so slight as to be imperceptible. However, there are occasions when in human presence the constant erosional process allows gravity to get the upper hand. This relentless force pulls down a great slab of stone, adding it to the talus slope and windblown sand while leaving on a canyon wall a fresh scar that was not there the day before.

But there *is* a Valley change readily visible, for it is almost sure to be a part of the daily routine. If the daytime scenario in Monument Valley is grand, the evening performance seldom fails to top it

The sandy stream bed of Canyon de Chelly is the roadless passageway for Navajo families who live in and farm the canyon. These same elusive tracks are followed by four-wheel-drive tours that show visitors the canyon's innermost wonders.

Mummy Cave Ruin in Canyon del Muerto's principal tributary to Canyon de Chelly is the largest of the many local cliff dwellings. Archaeological studies show this site to have been occupied over a thousand years—from the Basketmaker era to final desertion at the close of the Great Pueblo period.

Monument Valley

GARY LADD

The world-renowned Goulding's Trading Post & Lodge has come a long way from a tent-beginning over 60 years ago. Today, with completely modern lodging, dining, shopping, and Valley tour facilities, Goulding's is the perfect on-site headquarters for experiencing the sensational blend of natural scenic wonders and colorful Navajo culture that is Monument Valley.

Flamboyantly carved and colored buttes and monoliths, long shadows, and immensity of semiarid space dominate the Monument Valley scene. It does not take much imagination to understand how the Valley monuments received their descriptive names. The slender 460-foot-high "Totem Pole," the "Bear and the Rabbit," "Big Indian," "The Three Sisters," "Elephant Rock," and the "Mittens" are but a sampling. Scores of spectacular formations, some sheltering ancient ruins, rise as high as 1,200 feet above talus-slope bases. A host of natural arches like the "Sun's Eye" and the "Ear of the Wind" silently watch and listen as the drama of the ages drifts by.

The proud and colorful Navajo, at home in their traditional Valley hogans, add still another glorious touch. A little band of Navajo sheep driven down a wind-rippled sand dune, a Navajo on horseback, or a picturesque Navajo woman weaving a design in a wool rug against an imposing monument background—all are impressive highlights for Valley visitors' cameras and memories.

The magic spell of Monument Valley is not complete without a visit to the historic Goulding Trading Post. In 1923 Harry Goulding brought his young bride and a dream to this then roadless, lonely land. He named many of the monuments and befriended the Navajo. Later he introduced Monument Valley to the world by influencing Hollywood's John Ford to direct six major western epics there, starting with the Academy Award winning *Stagecoach,* which skyrocketed John Wayne to stardom.

Today a comfortable, complete, and modern lodge welcomes travelers. All guest rooms face incredible sunrise-to-sunset extravaganzas featuring an all-star monument cast. Additional local facilities include a modern market, gift shop, campground, school, and even a community hospital.

Drifting sand and towering stone spires like this Totem Pole and Yei-Bi-Chei Dancer formation make the setting that the Monument Valley Navajo call home. Velveteen dress, silver coin trim, and a touch of turquoise add Navajo color to an already multihued land.

JERRY JACKA

DAVID MUENCH

18

GARY LADD

Thunderbird Lodge in its parklike setting of green lawn and mature shade trees is a favorite stopover on the Grand Circle Adventure. This delightful oasis is conveniently located at the mouth of the enchanted land of Canyon de Chelly. Thunderbird Lodge is headquarters for lodging, dining, and fascinating four-wheel-drive tours into the heart of all the canyon-locked scenic splendor that extends right to the doorstep of ancient cliff dwellings and picturesque Navajo farms.

Canyon de Chelly

Canyon de Chelly's sheer and colorful sandstone walls soar a thousand feet to lock in a bountifully rich treasure chest of southwestern grandeur. Here, evidence of the Great Pueblo period is profusely and dramatically represented. It is an awesome sensation to peer over a lofty canyon rim and gaze hundreds of feet down upon ancient multiroom dwellings or onto strange rock formations such as Spider Rock, ascending nearly 900 feet skyward from the placid canyon floor. "White House," "Antelope House," and "Mummy Cave" cliff dwellings are but a few exceptional examples of Canyon de Chelly's once-thriving early "condominiums" that were deserted by the end of the thirteenth century.

Friendly, well-informed Navajo guides tell fascinating, authentic historical tales related to landmarks, caves, and ancient ruins visited on four-wheel-drive inner-canyon tours.

Between these colorful, rain-and-mineral-tapestried canyon walls, a shallow ribbon of water meanders along reflecting red sandstone and blue sky. Its border of venerable old cottonwoods adds a refreshing touch of summer green or shimmering gold in the fall. The sight and scent of fragrant blue wood smoke rising from log-and-earth hogans on little Navajo farms set a pleasant mood. A close-by corn and garden patch, a small cluster of lush peach trees, and perhaps a mare and colt in a verdant grassy pasture add to the already tranquil scene, much like a priceless, still-life painting.

Roadless canyon-bed sand prevents conventional car travel in the canyon. Heavy-duty four-wheel-drive commercial tour units with competent, informative driver-guides make entry to inner-canyon adventure, prehistoric ruins, and pictographs a delightful and simple matter.

Thunderbird Lodge at monument headquarters area excels in accommodations for rooms, dining, tours, and western welcome. Hospitality there adds greatly to visitor comfort and pleasure.

Canyon de Chelly must be experienced in person, for true feeling for and emotional fulfillment by its wall-to-wall splendor defy worthy description in mere words.

For reservations and information contact:
(Monument Valley) Goulding's Lodge, P. O. Box 1, Monument Valley, Utah 84536, 1-801-727-3231; (Canyon de Chelly) Thunderbird Lodge, P. O. Box 548, Chinle, Arizona 86503, 1-602-674-5443.

JOSEF MUENCH

Moccasin Arch, a sandstone halo above colorful Monument Valley Navajos.

JERRY JACKA

with an award-winning sunset sensation. Glowing monuments attempt to steal the scene while their shadows reach for miles across the sand, melting together at last to darken the entire valley floor.

Then comes the day's "grand finale." Night creeps up from the bases of the monuments to crowd the last orange rays of the sun off the tips of the already red sandstone buttes, firing them with an incandescence like molten copper that seems to radiate from within. Dusky monuments close the scene, standing in silent silhouette against a vari-colored violet, orange, and crimson sky. Night settling on the vast valley floor is disturbed only by two or three visible, widely separated Navajo campfires. All is well for another day.

A masterpiece of nature and much more, Monument Valley is a pleasing blend of sight, sound, and tranquility, and of Navajo culture and legend. It is an experience not to be forgotten . . . ever.

GOOSENECKS STATE RESERVE

From where the Goulding's–Monument Valley crossroad meets U.S. 163, it is 21 miles northeast on 163 to the San Juan River, which in this area is the northern border of the Navajo Reservation. Just across the bridge over the San Juan, a traveler's oasis on the east side of the highway got its name, "Mexican Hat," from a strange stone formation resembling an inverted *sombrero.* A buckled anticline, or roof-shaped fold of stratified earth crust, in the distant background is called the "Navajo Rug," after the weaving pattern it suggests.

About three miles farther north on U.S. 163,

Utah State Highway 261 branches to the left, heading for Goosenecks State Reserve. A mile ahead on Utah 261 a marked turnoff (Utah 316) leads west three miles to a canyon rim overlooking the San Juan River, deeply entrenched in its erosion-terraced abyss 1,500 feet below. At this point the river forms a series of tight "gooseneck" switchbacks as it meanders on its way to Lake Powell, transporting an estimated load over over 30 million tons of silt, sand, mud, and gravel each year.

To complete this scene a backdrop of Monument Valley monoliths serrates the distant skyline.

VALLEY OF THE GODS

After you return to Utah 261, it is five and a half miles north to a right-hand turnoff marked "Valley of the Gods." This side road is a fair-weather dirt loop 16 miles in length. The only sign of human habitation visible along this road is an old ranch house built by a grandson of Mormon pioneer and Colorado River ferryman John D. Lee.

The rest of the inhabitants of the valley are whatever your eyes make them out to be. For here is an enchanted playground for both the camera and the imagination. Sculptured stone columns and escarpments bring to mind objects from animals to stately "gods."

Monument Valley spires, splinters, buttes, mesas, and arches. These eroded remnants from a distant past were given names of the living, spiritual, or material things of which they were reminiscent. To the Navajo, one line of stony figures depicts the sacred "Yei-Bi-Chei" ceremonial dancers. The "Big Hogan" arch is related to Navajo creation. To the white man, the formations looked like: pancakes, an eye and an ear, a camel, a pioneer woman, a rooster, a stagecoach, and even wearing apparel like the well-known Mittens.

An incongruous pair: windswept sand dunes and a trickle of water. Not a green leaf nor a blade of grass, but still a pleasant sight to thirsty Navajos and their sheep. Sand Springs, a rare phenomenon in semiarid Monument Valley, surfaces, flows a few paces, then returns to the sand.

Where the Valley of the Gods loop road reaches U.S. 163, turn right, back toward Mexican Hat, four miles southwest. At the junction of U.S. 163 and 261, turn right on 261, this time bypassing both the Goosenecks and the Valley of the Gods turnoffs. You are on your way north to Natural Bridges National Monument.

You will not go far until you begin negotiating a series of hairpin switchbacks that elevate you several hundred feet to the crest of Cedar Mesa. If the switchbacks don't take your breath away, the view from an overlook just short of the top surely will. Below, the wide highway you have just traveled is but a thin thread reaching for the horizon. Let your eyes follow it into the distance, and you will have a pretty good idea of how well that often-used phrase "land of room enough and time enough" describes this part of the West.

Almost immediately after topping out on Cedar Mesa, you will encounter to the left a marked dirt road that leads five miles to Muley Point. Here is another spectacular lookout over a vast panorama of scoured-out San Juan canyon country, with the meandering river far below. Muley Point is a part of the Glen Canyon National Recreation Area. An interpretive display on the geology of the area is provided at this site.

DAVID MUENCH

21

This inverted "Mexican Hat" on the San Juan River in southern Utah marks a resort area and starting place for scenic tours and float trips to Lake Powell.

The placid mirror reflection 167 feet below Sipapu Bridge offers no hint of this stream's alternate personality of raging storm-fed torrents that carved this massive formation at Natural Bridges National Monument.

Valley of the Gods, an enchanting playground for both eye and camera. It takes little imagination to discover many sandstone-sculptured objects and animals. Near the entrance a huge organ grinder's monkey, complete with pillbox hat, welcomes you from a sleigh behind a Trojanlike horse. This 17-mile experience, just a little way off the beaten path, is a delightful adventure.

Goosenecks State Reserve overlooks a series of tight switchbacks in the San Juan River. Deeply entrenched in its terraced depths 1,500 feet below, this canyon-locked river slowly and relentlessly carves its way to the upper end of Lake Powell.

ALLEN C. REED

Natural Bridges National Monument

From Muley Point it is 28 miles north across the top of this grassy, juniper-covered plateau via Utah Highway 261 to Utah Highway 95. The prominent twin buttes to the north are called the "Bears Ears." The Abajo Mountains to the northeast are in the Manti-La Sal National Forest. After going two miles west on Utah 95, you will then take Utah Highway 275 for five miles to the visitor center and campground of Natural Bridges National Monument. This, the first national monument established in Utah, is open year-round.

A scenic eight-mile bridge-view drive from the visitor center takes in three massive natural bridges carved from Permian-age Cedar Mesa Sandstone. Viewing platforms overlooking each bridge are just steps away from designated parking areas. For hikers who feel the urge to take a whole lot more steps several miles of hiking trails connect all three.

Two of these bridges, Sipapu and Kachina, were scoured out by stream bed erosion. The third, Owachomo, on the side of the main stream bed, was carved mostly by rain, frost action, and sandblasting wind erosion. Information on the bridges and the area is available at the visitor center. A campground is located nearby.

Mesa Verde National Park

Your trip through the "Four Corners" country cannot be considered complete without a visit to the majestic plateau of Mesa Verde National Park and its matchless concentration of cliff dwellings. Mesa Verde is the classic example of prehistoric Indian architecture, and it provides a most enlightening insight into how these ancients conducted their everyday life.

To reach Mesa Verde from Natural Bridges, you will return on Utah 275 to Utah 95, then proceed eastward on 95 for 31 miles. From here you will turn south on U.S. 163-191 for 11 miles. At the junction you will follow Utah 262 first east, then south, then east again for a total of 31 miles. At Aneth, Utah, a partially paved, partially graded road takes you on a 40-mile drive through a picturesque farm belt in the canyon along the McElmo River. This lovely byway intersects U.S. 666-160 just 3 miles south of Cortez, Colorado. Approximately 11 miles east of Cortez on U.S. 160 is the entryway to Mesa Verde National Park.

From the park entrance a 21-mile scenic mountainous highway climbs over 1,600 feet while showing off distant desert topography and splendid vistas of six mountain ranges in four states. Lush farmland makes a crazy quilt of the Mancos River valley far below. Dropping down from an 8,572-foot summit to the 7,000-foot level of Mesa Verde, the highway leads to park headquarters in the heart of the homeland of this prehistoric civilization.

At the park headquarters museum you can marvel at the large collection of handsomely decorated pottery, baskets, tools, and other artifacts left behind when Mesa Verde's occupants vanished from the scene around 700 years ago. A series of authentically developed dioramas depict the evolution of Anasazi ("the ancient ones") culture. These dramatic miniature displays, complete with inhabitants involved in their everyday way of life, can take the imagination back over a thousand years in time to when this Stone-Age civilization flourished. The dioramas range from the Basketmaker period of the sixth century through the Great Pueblo period from A.D. 1100 to 1300. The cliff-dweller period itself lasted less than 100 years. It is thought that before the close of the thirteenth century severe drought and other causes drove these people from their homes forever, as it did the inhabitants at Hovenweep, now a national monument, some 30 miles to the west.

The largest and one of the best-preserved cliff dwellings in the Southwest is Mesa Verde's Cliff Palace. It is sheltered by a cave 325 feet wide, 60 feet high, and 90 feet deep. Standing at the edge of a Mesa Verde cliff and looking down across a narrow canyon at Cliff Palace, you can imagine the thrill that cowboys Richard Wetherill and Charles Mason felt when they discovered Mesa Verde in 1888.

However, the height of fascination is likely to be the close-up experience of actually strolling

through some of these well-preserved dwellings of the ancients with an informative ranger-guide. There are scores of known sites in a variety of sizes and conditions preserved in the shielding cliff depressions of numerous mesa side canyons. Some of the better known and most often seen have descriptive names like "Square Tower House," "Spruce Tree House," "Long House," and "Balcony House." Ranger-conducted tours will take you into a number of them. Along the roads of the mesa-top ruins you can clearly see the sequence of prehistoric architectural development from pithouses to kivas.

A visit to the museum, park-service information packets, roadside exhibits, guided and self-guided tours, and summer evening campfire talks by rangers all contribute to the pleasure and understanding of the ancient inhabitants of this 52,000-acre park area. Food, lodging, camping, and bus tours are available in the park from early May to late October. The park headquarters and museum are open throughout the winter months.

CANYONLANDS NATIONAL PARK— NEEDLES DISTRICT

To reach the Needles district of Canyonlands National Park from Mesa Verde, return to Cortez, then take U.S. 666 north. For these next 60 miles the highway passes through rolling farmland on the way to Monticello, Utah. Nearly 15 miles north of Monticello on U.S. 163-191, a lone light-colored Entrada Sandstone butte with a red sandstone base juts up on the east side of the road. This is "Church Rock," sometimes referred to as the "Wine Jug" because of its juglike shape, with an imaginary little bit of red wine left at the bottom.

On the opposite side of the highway from this lone landmark, Utah Highway 211 leads west through 38 miles of scenic canyon country to the "Needles District" in the southern section of Canyonlands National Park. About 12 miles in, the roadway cuts through Indian Creek State Park and passes close to one of the best-preserved and most intriguing collections of petroglyphs in the Southwest. This flat Wingate Sandstone formation is known as "Newspaper Rock." Aged with a blackened coat of natural mineral stain (iron oxide) called "desert varnish," it is covered with hundreds of impressions pecked into its surface. It is estimated that the numerous inscriptions and figures cut into the sandstone cliff probably span a thousand years. They include figures made by prehistoric Indians and those made more recently by Utes and a few early white settlers.

As you head west through a variety of colorful canyon formations, along the last 19 miles into the Needles area two historical landmarks, North and South Sixshooter peaks, are plainly visible on the skyline. Another unusual sandstone formation against the skyline farther on is a fairly good

Preceding pages: Visitors to Mesa Verde tread in the footsteps of the ancients on a ranger-conducted tour of Mesa Verde's Cliff Palace. Photo by David Muench.

DAVID MUENCH

Circular subterranean kivas found in ancient cliff dwellings of the Southwest were entered by ladder through a roof hatchway like those in the stone-paved courtyard of Spruce Tree House (above). Typical kiva interiors, like the one uncovered at Mug House (right), contained a central fire pit, a ventilator shaft with draft baffle in front, and an encircling masonry shelf with roof-support pilasters. The ceremonial kiva, evolving from an earlier pithouse society, became an integral part of religious and social clan structure of the Great Pueblo period.

replica of a giant wooden shoe. Approximately 32 miles from U.S. 163-191 you reach the park boundary.

The drama of Canyonlands National Park, with its surrealistic 525-square-mile maze of meandering canyons, swirls of candy-striped sandstone fins, bristling forests of towering monoliths, gravity-defying balanced rocks, and graceful arches could be billed as 300 million years in the making. Altogether it is an explorer's utopia by foot, horseback, river, air, or four-wheel-drive vehicle with a local guide.

Just outside the eastern boundary of the park is Canyonlands Resort where groceries, gasoline, trailer hookups, tours, and charter flights are available. A short distance into the park is the contact station, which provides information about the area, the campground, and other facilities. It is not far from here to the highway's end amid a cluster of colorful spires and pinnacles—outposts of the vast, mysterious badlands beyond.

If standing on the outside looking in is not enough, and if you are physically up to it, you can load your backpack with necessary supplies in-

cluding maps, camera, and film and hike in. It is also possible to arrange a horseback pack trip.

The best bet is a four-wheel-drive vehicle, but the going can be pretty rough with some 40 percent grades and backup switchbacks. However, your rewards and those of your camera will be many, for hidden throughout this remote sandstone labyrinth are scores of fantastic natural formations. Names of some of the better known, like "Angel Arch," "Wedding Ring Arch," "Caterpillar Arch," "Washerwoman," "Walls of Jericho," "Moses and Zeus," and "Paul Bunyan's Potty," may offer some descriptive clues to their bizarre appearance.

The easiest way to obtain an overall view, although you sacrifice the close-up detail, is to arrange for a scenic flight. Local inquiries at the Canyonlands Resort and at Moab and Monticello should lead to some interesting adventures in this treasure trove of wild and wonderful banded sandstone formations.

ARCHES NATIONAL PARK

When you return from the Needles District to U.S. 163-191, you will drive 39 miles north to Moab, Utah. Located on the Colorado River, this community is a next-door neighbor to Arches National Park. Moab is one of the largest business-supply centers on this Grand Circle Adventure. The 4,000-foot Moab Valley is rich in scenery, minerals, and signs of the prehistoric past—from dinosaur tracks imbedded in sandstone to Anasazi ruins. From here you can arrange for a float trip down the Colorado River—another way to come to know this powerful country.

The gateway to Arches National Park is approximately six miles north of Moab on U.S. 163-191. A paved highway takes you to viewpoints and trail heads from which hikers can reach the most spectacular of the 200 known arches in this 114-square-mile gallery of nature's magnificent masterpieces. Again the elements have run rampant: sculpturing, balancing, and painting majestic murals.

Visualize a slim, graceful horizontal stone span, chiseled from an enormous sandstone "fin" nearly 300 feet long, weighing thousands of tons, and tapering down to a thickness of a mere 6 feet at one end. This is Landscape Arch, the longest known natural arch in the world. To stand in its presence—but not *under* it, unless you have nerves of steel—requires an easy mile hike from a parking area. But take along a wide-angle lens if you want to get both ends in your picture. The well-constructed trail to Landscape Arch, and one more mile beyond, rewards the hiker with views of six natural arches.

Another fascinating arch, just steps away from a parking area, is Double Arch. The larger of the two openings could accommodate a 15-story building with room to spare.

Perhaps the best known and most photographed formation in Arches National Park is Delicate Arch. This majestic natural wonder can be observed in

The prominent four-story structure that dominates Square Tower House was not originally a tower. Second- and third-story walls of adjoining dwellings have fallen away, leaving this tallest Mesa Verde ruin to stand alone.

the distance from a viewpoint on the east side of the park. However, the most spectacular view of it requires a somewhat demanding mile-and-a-half hike that climbs 500 feet from the historic Wolfe Ranch area of the park. The Wolfe Ranch was homesteaded in 1888 by a Civil War veteran. A time-worn log cabin, a corral, and the remains of a wagon are all that is left by the side of the trail to Delicate Arch.

It would be difficult to surpass the stately splendor of Delicate Arch as it stands alone, both feet planted firmly on the crest of its own private sandstone amphitheater. But when the nearby La Sal Mountain range is snowcapped behind this majestic red sandstone frame, and when sun and sky and clouds act out their roles, the ultimate in nature's dramatic artistry is unveiled.

Arches National Park is open to visitors year-round as are lodging and supply centers in Moab. On your trip to Arches don't miss the visitor cen-

Cliff Palace, the largest of the preserved Mesa Verde cliff dwellings, is a classic example of Great Pueblo culture. Its 200 rooms and 23 clan kivas were once a part of the life-style of over 200 people. Here in the cliff dwellings and mesa-top pueblos, refinements in architecture, farming, pottery, and textile weaving reached their "Golden Age," only to be lost forever when the mesa was completely and inexplicably deserted at the close of the thirteenth century.

Of the scores of once-occupied mesa-top pueblos, most have crumbled under the relentless battering of the ages. Mysterious Sun Temple, thought to be a carefully planned ceremonial structure, is one of the few surface ruins still partly standing.

A big plus in visiting national parks on the Grand Circle Adventure is the ever present convenience and comfort of quality concessionaire accommodations. After an exciting day hiking the trails into Mesa Verde's past, it's a well-earned pleasure to kick off your shoes and relax in a comfortable room with a view. Far View Lodge in Mesa Verde has it all: view, dining room, lounge, cocktail lounge, and meeting rooms. A cafeteria, gift shop, service station, tour terminal, campground, campstore, and visitor-center museum are close by.

GARY LADD

Mesa Verde

It was December 18, 1888. From a Colorado ranch near Mancos, two cowboys, Richard Wetherill and Charles Mason, rode to the top of a wild, tree-covered mesa in search of strays. Looking down into a hidden side canyon, their eyes fell upon a startling sight. Sheltered in a deep cliffside alcove was an immense centuries-old cliff dwelling.

Upon exploring some of the 200 rooms, Wetherill and Mason discovered that its erstwhile inhabitants had left in a hurry and had been gone a long, long time. Orderly placement of handsome, decorated black-on-white pottery, corrugated clay cookware, tools, farming implements, weapons, and other articles of everyday life that had not been totally covered by dust of the ages gave an impression that the departed owners had intended to come right back. But, in fact, they had been gone nearly 600 years.

This mysterious dwelling was named Cliff Palace. It proved to be the largest of its kind in the entire Southwest. The cave that shelters it is 325 feet wide, up to 60 feet high, and as much as 90 feet deep. But Cliff Palace was only the beginning. Further exploration led to similar finds at hundreds of lesser sites in fringe-area canyons as well as at numerous Pueblo ruins on the mesa top.

By 1906 Mesa Verde was established as a national park. Cliff Palace, Spruce Tree House, and Balcony House are considered the finest examples of cliff dwellings found anywhere in North America. They are prime specimens of the Great Pueblo period, when improved techniques in architecture, farming, pottery, arts, crafts and water- and soil-conservation methods of the Anasazi, who had occupied them, had reached their culmination. This peak was the Golden Age of Pueblo culture. Then suddenly it was over, for what reasons no one is entirely certain. Perhaps there was a combination of pressures such as outside enemy harrassment or threat of starvation during an unbearably severe 14-year local drought at that time.

Until the late nineteenth century discovery of these ancient mesa homes, where hundreds of Anasazi families had once built and farmed and struggled to survive, many seasons had come and gone—more than 550 since their firepits had grown cold. Only the sounds of nature and the song of the wind were left to break the silence while lonely pueblos stared from empty hollow-eyed windows at centuries of solitude.

Daily tours are conducted through these major dwellings. Interpretive fireside chats, rim-view drives, exceptionally detailed museum dioramas, and displays of hundreds of artifacts recovered from the ruins weave a fascinating tale.

It is quite obvious to guests of mesa-top Far View Lodge why present-day Indians call Mesa Verde the "land of the far look." From each terrace of the 150 guest rooms the spectacular "far look" reaches deep into four states. New Mexico's commanding Shiprock punctuates the view to the south. The Blue Mountains and 75-mile-distant twin mesas called "Bears Ears" add Utah to the scene. From the

GARY LADD

To enhance your Mesa Verde experience, find a few moments to sit quietly at a cliff-dwelling overlook and turn your thoughts deep into the past. How much ancient drama can pass your mind's eye while you contemplate the imaginary scene at that exact spot 700 years ago when activity was in full bloom?

JERRY JACKA

comfort of your terrace or room your vision can wander from the "Four Corners Country" of Arizona to four lofty mountain ranges in western Colorado.

It is also evident to visitors why the Lodge has a fine reputation of dining excellence. It is a property of specialists in food: ARA, Inc., food service company for the Olympics.

Mesa Verde both past and present is one more never-to-be-forgotten experience on the Grand Circle Adventure.

For reservations and information contact:
ARA Mesa Verde Co., Far View Lodge in Mesa Verde,
P. O. Box 277, Mancos, Colorado 81328, 1-303-529-4421

Long House, the second largest Mesa Verde ruin, occupies an immense cliffside alcove on Wetherill Mesa.

DAVID MUENCH

DAVID MUENCH

The stature of man is diminished in size in the presence of Angel Arch deep in the Salt Creek area of rugged Canyonlands National Park. Angel Arch is considered by many who have seen it to be one of the most beautiful of all arches anywhere.

JEFF GNASS

ter, which offers a wealth of interesting geological, historical, and general information about the area.

DEAD HORSE POINT STATE PARK

After returning from Arches to U.S. 163-191, you will travel only six miles north before you encounter Utah Highway 313 to your left. Approximately 14 miles west of this turnoff, the marked, paved highway continues southeast 22 miles to Dead Horse Point State Park.

Dead Horse Point overlooks a magnificent sweep of spectacular canyon lands including a loop in the Colorado River nearly 2,000 feet down. The erosion-terraced canyon walls expose layer upon layer of sandstone, mudstone, conglomerate, and limestone formations laid down between 200 million and 300 million years of intermittent overflow and departure of shallow inland seas. Relentless natural forces of erosion took their time in carving the terrain below as the river washed thousands of cubic miles of rock, silt, and sand sediments into an ancient sea.

Just before arriving at the tip of Dead Horse Point, the highway passes through a narrowed neck that almost isolates the point from the rest of the plateau. In the early days of western settlement, bands of wild horses that roamed the plateau were driven toward the point by local cowboys. A short fence across the narrow strip was all that was needed to trap the horses in a natural corral between the sheer cliffs until the better ones could be sorted out and sold. As the story goes, one band of horses corralled too long died for lack of water, thus creating the name that this promontory still carries.

Where the highway enters the park you will find a visitor center, a museum, modern campgrounds, and picnic facilities. On the horizon the distant La Sal Mountains provide a splendid background.

CANYONLANDS NATIONAL PARK— ISLAND IN THE SKY DISTRICT

On your way back from Dead Horse Point you will notice an unpaved road off to your left. It leads to the "Island in the Sky" district of Canyonlands National Park. You can view the north section of this park from a 6,000-foot-high bench plateau separating the Green River and the Colorado River canyons.

The ranger station at the park entrance will provide visitors with folders that include maps and information on mileage, campgrounds, trails, and

JEFF GNASS

*From the magic that holds up Balanced Rock
to the majestic sensation of Delicate Arch,
the intense drama of light, shadow, color, and
form at Arches National Park is staged
to please the most demanding critic.*

*Below Canyonland's "Island in the Sky"
a layer of White Rim Sandstone atop the
Organ Rock Tongue Formation stands out like
icing on a devil's food cake.*

DAVID MUENCH

Spectacles on a snub-nosed, ragged-toothed gargoyle? See whatever you will in nature's gallery of monuments at Arches.

points of scenic interest. Some of the more prominent features are "Green River Overlook" and "Upheaval Dome." "Grand View Point" at the far southern tip of the plateau overlooks a vast gouged-out basin of red organlike rock spires and cliffs capped with white rim sandstone reminiscent of sugar icing on a chocolate cake. In the distance the Needles district of Canyonlands lies almost due south of Grand View Point. After you have absorbed the wild beauty of this remote area, you will return along the unpaved road to Utah 313, then proceed northeast to U.S. 163-191.

Goblin Valley State Reserve

From the intersection with Utah 313, you drive 21 miles north to where U.S. 163-191 meet Interstate 70. West on I-70 35 miles, Utah Highway 24 heads south to the Goblin Valley area on its way to Hanksville. About 25 miles south on Utah 24, a paved road marked "Goblin Valley State Reserve" intersects from the west. Five miles in on this road a signed, graded dirt road heading southwest takes you the last seven miles to a wide secluded valley. Its hard-packed, sunbaked floor is populated with thousands of standing rocks of Entrada Sandstone, sculptured by nature and resembling almost every type of goblinlike creature your wildest imagination will allow.

Strolling amidst the goblins' grotesque forms, you can easily lose hours discovering and photographing. There are giants over 50 feet tall down through man-size to stony little trolls. There are those with long noses and those with short noses; some stand alone; some are apparently seriously engrossed in conference. And there is no shortage of their stony pets: animals from caterpillars to Donald Duck. Goblin Valley is a name well chosen for this fascinating fantasyland where you and your camera will have a field day.

Although there are a few four-wheel-drive roads in the area, there is not much choice for a conventional car but to backtrack to Utah 24, then turn south for about 20 miles and cross the Dirty Devil River to Hanksville en route to Capitol Reef.

From Hanksville you can take an interesting side trip southeast on Utah 95 to Hite Marina at the upper end of Lake Powell.

Capitol Reef National Park

West from Hanksville, Utah 24 follows the scenic Fremont River canyon past several marked points of historical interest some 30 miles to the colorful towering cliffs and deep canyons of Capitol Reef National Park. This region is the heart of some of the last territory to be explored in the continental United States (around the mid-1800s). In 1937, 3,700 acres were set aside as Capitol Reef National Monument. It was not until 1971 that an act of the U.S. Congress changed its status to that of a national park and enlarged the boundaries.

Capitol Reef is a sensation in geological formation, color, history, and wildlife. Early Native

In leaving behind strange forms, erosion plays many whimsical tricks. Here in the Fisher Towers area, not far from Arches National Park, an imaginary dinosaur rears its fierce stony head.

Americans called this canyon country "Land of the Sleeping Rainbow" because of the variegated outcrops of Chinle Shale that stretch like a sprawling rainbow along the base of the cliffs. The name of this 241,271-acre park was inspired by massive grayish-white domes eroded from a layer of Navajo Sandstone 1,000 feet thick. These forms were thought to be reminiscent of the dome of the nation's Capitol.

The "Reef" part of the park's name was applied to the massive barrierlike "S"-shaped upthrust fold in the earth's crust called the "Waterpocket Fold." This descriptive term comes from numerous natural tanks and potholes that hold huge quantities of rainwater in the spring. The extreme subterranean pressures that wrinkled the earth's crust into the fold exposed the edges of at least seven different layers of geological formations, laid one on top of another, over a period of 250 million years. This gigantic upheaval of majestic domes, sheer multicolored escarpments, and deeply eroded canyons extends nearly a hundred miles from the north

GARY LADD

Over millions of years relentless natural forces of erosion carved the terracelike canyon scene spread out beneath Dead Horse Point. A gooseneck loop in the Colorado River is nearly 2,000 feet straight down. A thread of the four-wheel-drive Shafer Trail, constructed during the uranium boom of the 1950s, meanders below.

ALLEN C. REED

You can't afford to be self-conscious in the haunts of Goblin Valley, for the hundreds of little people and their strange pets keep a wary watch on your every move.

JEFF GNASS

The 726-foot steel arch on Utah State Highway 95 at Hite crosses the Colorado River arm of Lake Powell 141 scenic miles up lake from Glen Canyon Dam.

end of the park south beyond the Bullfrog Basin section of Lake Powell.

Visitors can spend days hiking the local trails or making side trips into a variety of nearby scenic and historic locations. Places with highly appropriate or historic names include "Cathedral Valley," "Capitol Gorge," "Cohab Canyon," "Cassidy Arch," and "Golden Throne."

Zane Grey's novel *Robbers' Roost* was inspired by the maze of blind canyons and hidden trails in this remote area, once a favorite haunt of Butch Cassidy, "The Sundance Kid," "Big Nose" George Curry, and the rest of the "Wild Bunch." These notorious Old-West outlaws used this rugged canyon country as an escape route or as a hideout after relieving a bank, train, or mine paymaster of cash on hand. Knowing intimately every trail and water hole in these badlands made eluding a knowledgeable posse a simple matter.

A number of books and movies have been produced to immortalize this setting. Some of the better-known novels, in addition to *Robbers' Roost,* are Pearl Baker's *The Wild Bunch* and Charles Kelly's *The Outlaw Trail.* Paul Newman and Robert Redford helped keep the legends alive in the movie *Butch Cassidy and the Sundance Kid.* The old homestead cabin in which Butch Cassidy grew up still stands about 60 air miles west of the visitor center near Circleville, Utah, on U.S. 89.

The Capitol Reef visitor center on Sulphur Creek is a lush oasis in this rather barren canyon country. The center is located in a verdant valley of pastureland and fruit orchards walled in by towering cliffs. This site was farmed by early Mormon pioneer families.

From Capitol Reef, Utah 24 leads to a turnoff less than a mile east of the town of Torrey, located ten miles to the west. From here Utah Highway 12, or Boulder Mountain Road, offers a scenic shortcut of a little over 100 miles southward to Bryce Canyon, the next national park on our circuit. A large segment of Utah 12 is unpaved, and the highway is closed in winter.

BRYCE CANYON NATIONAL PARK

The first 38 miles, to the quiet little farming community of Boulder, pass through part of the Dixie National Forest and across scenic, forested Boulder Mountain—9,200 feet high at its summit. In spring and summer the grassy meadows are a sea of wildflowers. Golden aspen shimmer among dark stately pines in fall. As you near the summit and look east through occasional breaks in the stand of timber, you can glimpse Capitol Reef and Waterpocket Fold in the distance below.

Boulder, with a population of less than 100, is a delight to see. At the north edge of Boulder are the Anasazi Indian Village State Historical Monument and a museum. A collection of artifacts and information makes a visit here well worthwhile in helping round out your knowledge and understanding of the prehistoric Indian culture that

occupied the Colorado Plateau country so many centuries ago.

From Boulder, Utah 12 winds approximately 74 miles through the little pioneer Mormon (Latter-Day Saint) settlements of Escalante, Henrieville, Cannonville, and Tropic to a well-marked turnoff onto Utah Highway 63 to the south and the headquarters of Bryce Canyon National Park. Most of these picturesque towns look much the same as they did two or three generations ago.

Bryce Canyon received its name from an early Mormon pioneer, Ebenezer Bryce, who settled in the area, built a cabin, and claimed grazing rights. His often-quoted, best-remembered description of Bryce Canyon was: "a hell of a place to lose a cow!" Because he ran cattle in the area, his statement probably carried a note of authentic, firsthand experience.

Until you park your car and walk to the rim of the canyon, you are in a ponderosa, spruce, fir, and aspen forest typical of this 8,000-foot altitude. Then, when you emerge from the forest at the edge of the Pink Cliffs, you face a vast expanse of delicate, intricately eroded, multicolored minarets, spires, and pinnacles that, by the thousands, make up the lacy fretwork of the striking badland topography below.

Most of the geological formations you have seen

DAVID MUENCH

A magnificent extravaganza of wild geological display and vivid color: that is Capitol Reef National Park. From the regal splendor of Cathedral Valley (left) majestic domes, towering cliffs, mysterious canyons, and hidden pools stretch 70 miles south to Lake Powell's Bullfrog Basin. All this color in the "Land of the Sleeping Rainbow" is seasonally accented from a riot of spring wildflowers through summer green to the golden rewards of fall (right).

so far on this adventure were carved from solidified sands and sediments laid down 125 million to 250 million years ago. Comparatively, Bryce Canyon National Park is a rank newcomer, dating back a mere 60 million years.

To set the first stage, powerful subterranean forces thrust surrounding land slightly higher than the present Bryce terrain, causing watercourses to drain inland, dumping a wide variety and vast volume of silt and mud sediments into huge inland lakes. The buoyancy of the water provided a natural sorting process. Coarse materials dropped out first where the rivers entered the lakes. In the deepest water a limey ooze settled to the bottom and hardened into stone.

Later, with more intermittent regional shifting, a final uplift of the present Bryce area drained the lakes for the last time and exposed the solidified sediments. More shifts of the earth's crust followed, along with ever-present erosion. This relatively soft, less stable material was broken and sculptured into the delicate, colorful columns that make Bryce Canyon the exotic expression of nature's art that it is today.

The Capitol Reef area is loaded with historical remnants of a pioneer past, like this weathered old mill near Teasdale, Utah.

There are a number of rim-drive viewpoints of these pastel-tinted monuments. In addition, a series of trails invites you to wander down among the delicately carved corridors and palisades of the inner canyons. But if the altitude of Bryce seems a little high for extended hikes, you can take one of the horseback trips conducted each morning and afternoon through the summer season. You can make arrangements at Bryce Canyon Lodge in the park.

Located close to the rim, Bryce Canyon Lodge offers both lodging and food from mid-May to mid-October. At two sites within the park camping may be enjoyed from around mid-May into October. Food and lodging are available outside the park on a year-around basis.

Cedar Breaks National Monument

The next trail on your adventure leads 21 miles northwest, via Utah Highway 12 and U.S. 89, down 1,000 feet through the pines, silver-green sage, and bluffs of Red Canyon to Panguitch, Utah. From Panguitch a paved county road climbs 3,000 feet to an altitude of 10,000 feet in the Dixie National Forest. The highway skirts Panguitch Lake and winds 32 miles through majestic forests of pine, spruce, and quaking aspen and through rolling green mountain meadows—all of which are garnished with wildflowers during spring and summer.

You have slipped into Cedar Breaks National Monument by the "back door" on the north end. You will not reach the visitor center until you are about to leave by the front door at the southern boundary of the monument. Four miles north of where you entered the park is Brian Head Resort. A delightful mountain setting with many summer homes, it is best known as one of the Southwest's most popular ski resorts. Groceries and gasoline are available here.

When you arrive at the canyon rim, you will find a gigantic multihued amphitheater spread out at your feet. Although the origin, composition, and coloring of Cedar Breaks are much the same as those of the Pink Cliffs of Bryce Canyon, you will find that this entire ten-square-mile monument has a physical character, a personality, and a beauty all its own.

Here, as in many other areas of the West, the juniper trees were erroneously referred to as "cedars" by the early settlers. This misnomer, combined with their common use of the word "breaks" in referring to badlands, resulted in the "Cedar Breaks" name.

There are a number of inviting rim trails and forest trails in the monument, but no trails lead down to the bottom of Cedar Breaks. A five-mile rim drive reaches four major viewpoints, each offering a different panorama of the Breaks and the Utah high-country background sweeping away toward the distant mountainous skyline. A visitor center, campground, and picnic area are the extent of the accommodations.

DAVID MUENCH

From easy-to-reach overlooks on the forest-lined rim highway to strange sights from hikers' isolated viewpoints, there is a world of sensational splendor to be experienced at Bryce. Seven trails from 1½ to 28 miles long skirt the rim above and below or penetrate deep into the labyrinth of narrow inner corridors of an enchanted fantasyland.

Leaving Cedar Breaks by the southern route (Utah 143) and turning east on Utah Highway 14, you will then head 23 miles back to U.S. 89. Several signs marking side roads along this stretch refer to places such as Aspen Mirror Lake, Cascade Falls, and Navajo Lake.

Zion National Park

From Long Valley Junction, where Utah 14 meets U.S. 89, it is 22 miles south to Mount Carmel Junction. From here Utah Highway 9 (formerly also Utah 15) travels west 23 miles to Zion National Park. This approach to Zion meanders through immense sandstone formations that originated millions of years ago as gigantic wind-deposited sand dunes that were later covered over and compressed into stone. They will give you a modest clue as to what is to be seen at Zion.

En route to Zion Canyon, Utah 9 passes through two tunnels, one more than a mile long. Just before the second and longer tunnel, on the right (or north) side the Canyon Overlook Trail leads up a half mile to a magnificent view of the west side of Zion and the looping ribbon of the Zion–Mount Carmel highway entering the canyon far below. It

DAVID MUENCH

A nineteenth-century government surveyor called Bryce Canyon "the wildest, most wonderful scene the eye of man ever beheld." To a geologist the Pink Cliffs of Bryce were "a brilliant jewel in a land of superb texture and workmanship." Paiute Indians saw the stony sentinels as "red rocks standing like men in a bowl-shaped canyon." By 1928 Bryce had been extolled in so many ways that the U.S. Congress, convinced it was one of the world's most intricately eroded and strikingly beautiful examples of badlands topography, made it a national park. Bryce is really two different worlds: the heavily forested 8,000-foot plateau at the park entrance and lodge, and the totally different wonderworld below the rim where hundreds of formations, like the Queen Victoria sculpture (left), have unique personalities of their own.

A valiant pine exhibiting a courageous, unconquered tenacity.

Weeping Rock, a natural alcove curtained by constantly falling water droplets that sparkle like tiny jewels in the sun, is just one of many easy-to-reach features at Zion National Park.

park you can see a great deal right from the highway. Tree-framed impressions of immense erosion-carved sandstone formations thrusting hundreds of feet upward are viewed from different perspectives at every turn. Nature's colorful megaliths, with names like "Great White Throne," "Court of the Patriarchs," "Mountain of the Sun," "The Sentinel," and "Angels Landing," tower over the highway on the canyon floor.

As you stand deeply immersed in admiration of the Zion scene, the relentless drama of erosion goes on imperceptibly right before your eyes. It is estimated that at present the Virgin River removes more than a million tons of rock and sand from the canyon each year. The major portion is transported during extensive snowmelt or massive thunderstorm-caused flooding.

Complementing the park's striking views and points of interest are many hiking trails. There are nearly a dozen maintained trails, rated from easy to strenuous, which lead to East Rim, West Rim, Emerald Pools, Weeping Rock, Hidden Canyon, Angels Landing, Watchman Viewpoint, Sand Bench, and Kolob Arch.

Footpaths lead to some of the more remote areas of this fascinating park. One mile-long path, for example, goes from the parking area at the Temple of Sinawava along the Virgin River to the spectacular Gateway to The Narrows and the Hanging Gardens of Zion.

Arrangements for guided horseback excursions on some of the trails and for highway tours of the park can be made at Zion Lodge. Meals and lodging are also available at Zion Lodge and in the small town of Springdale on Utah 9 just outside the park to the west.

Weathering along weaker horizontal and vertical planes of this ancient sand dune creates the biscuit effect of Checkerboard Mesa near the east entrance of Zion.

Autumn in a world of canyon contrasts. Zion's Great White Throne and Angels Landing with colors muted by misty blue distance and shadow.

is an interesting, easy walk to this point and well worth the hour round trip. If you pick up a trail guide at the start of the trail, it will give you a very concise, step-by-step layman's education on the geology, plants, birds, and animal life of the area.

After passing through the long tunnel and driving down the winding loops that you saw from the overlook, you will encounter to the right the Zion Canyon turnoff that follows along the North Fork of the Virgin River for six miles. This road will take you to the Zion Lodge and campground. Beyond the lodge a few miles the road terminates in a parking area deep in the bottom of the canyon. However, if you continue on a short distance *past* this turnoff straight ahead on Utah 9, you will come to Zion's visitor center. The center offers area maps; information; and exhibits on geology, natural history, and other topics related to the park. Illustrated interpretive talks on the park are presented each evening at the lodge and campgrounds.

Unlike the more fragile, ornamental spires of Bryce, Zion is overwhelmingly massive and seems to engulf the valley below. When you tour this

PIPE SPRING NATIONAL MONUMENT

Leaving Zion the same way you came in, you will backtrack east on Utah 9 to Mount Carmel Junction and U.S. 89, then continue south on U.S. 89, 17 miles to Kanab, Utah, one of the larger towns on the circuit.

Kanab is an early Mormon settlement. It is well worth spending a little time driving along a few back streets and looking at some of the picturesque architecture of fine old southern Utah homes.

Just seven miles south of Kanab on U.S. Alternate 89 (89A), which crosses the border into Arizona, is the town of Fredonia. Here Arizona Highway 389 cuts off to the west 14 miles to Pipe Spring National Monument on the Kaibab-Paiute Indian Reservation. Pipe Spring was discovered in 1858 by a group of Mormon missionaries from Indiana. In 1865 Dr. James Whitmore started a livestock ranch here. Bands of Navajo raiders forced the abandonment of Pipe Spring in 1866.

In 1870 Mormon leader Brigham Young reestablished a ranch at Pipe Spring for raising cattle and production of dairy products for nearby settlements. A stone-block fort typical of Mormon

41

Zion Lodge in the magnificent heart of Zion National Park, like Bryce Canyon Lodge and Grand Canyon Lodge, makes an ideal vacation headquarters. Dining, lodging, and tour accommodations of all three are of the high caliber that is to be expected from their responsible, professional operator, TWA Services, Inc.

GARY LADD

Regularly scheduled horseback rides with qualified wranglers may be arranged at Bryce, Zion, and Grand Canyon lodges. Each park ride offers a totally different experience. The Bryce ride winds deep into an enchanted stone forest of ethereal brilliance. Zion winds 3,000 feet heavenward for matchless views. Grand Canyon's horseback ride follows the rim. By muleback you will go deep down into the Canyon to Roaring Springs. Each ride is an exciting, never-to-be-forgotten adventure.

DICK DIETRICH

ED COOPER

A 28-mile round-trip bus tour from the North Rim's Grand Canyon Lodge to Point Imperial and Cape Royal offers different canyon perspectives. A geology talk is included. Angels Window, a natural bridge near Cape Royal, frames a third imposing canyon view.

Bryce Canyon National Park

Layer upon layer of silts, sands, muds, and shale comprise the raw material for the work of art known as Bryce Canyon. Rain, snow, heat, frost, and wind were nature's sculpting tools. Iron oxide in varying concentrations blended with manganese and other minerals to provide the colorful palette. It then took something like 60 million years to create the masterpiece. To delight in its splendor today is to peek over the shoulder of the elements still at work, for such geological artistry is never completed; it simply goes on and on.

Looking down into Bryce Canyon from the rim is hardly enough. To experience its full glory you should try it on from the inside. An inviting web of foot trails loops through its mysterious inner sanctum of the unexpected. Here, surrounded by fanciful figures towering hundreds of feet overhead, is a totally different adventure in color and perspective. Intimacy with fluted layers of pinks, corals, golds, lavenders, rusts, and leached white creates a magic fantasy-world all its own. Bryce is not all arches, windows, statues, and fretworks in stone, however, for hidden among its trailside surprises are little parks carpeted with grass and wildflowers and framed by a sprinkling of tall pines.

At the visitor center near the park entrance you can learn a lot about the geology, natural history, wildlife, recreation, and activities at Bryce. Just steps from the rim, Bryce Canyon Lodge makes an ideal headquarters for a vacation stay. Motel facilities outside the park are open year-round.

Zion National Park

Zion National Park: 206 square miles of rugged wilderness where the Virgin River has cut a notch well over half a mile deep—right down the middle. In the northern section there is a notch so narrow that a hiker with outstretched arms can, in places, reach halfway across the canyon. Near the Temple of Sinawava, the river, tired of playing in hidden passages, widened the canyon into the glorious six-mile-long showcase that is now the heartland of Zion.

All of this work makes the Virgin River sound formidable. It is an up-country cloudburst that writes a violent scenario, flushing something like a half-million cubic yards of silt and rock through the canyon in one day. Yet on an average day you will find the river softly gurgling along, the laughter of children drifting up from a favorite swimming hole, and horses splashing across it with park visitors off on a trail ride.

Possibly the greatest six-mile highway of concentrated scenic magnificence anywhere winds beside the Virgin River with magnificent temples, thrones, and domes towering 2,000 to 3,000 feet overhead. Ten trails, from a half mile to 12 miles in length, reach fascinating places of awesome beauty. There are a lot of delightful adventures to experience at Zion, and right in the middle of the canyon, under huge shade trees surrounded by attractive green lawns, is rustic Zion Lodge—the perfect starting place to help make it all happen.

JOSEF MUENCH

Grand Canyon Lodge, perched on Bright Angel Point, presents the Canyon to its guests in many ways. They can thrill to the Canyon's serene magnificence through picture windows or from a spacious patio or from forward viewpoints on the canyon brink.

Grand Canyon National Park—North Rim

More than nine out of ten visitors to the Grand Canyon have missed out on one of the most delightful chapters of its stately grandeur by not including in their travels the more isolated North Rim. A refreshingly new dimension awaits those who have not yet enjoyed the different world of the 1,000-foot-higher Kaibab Plateau. At first sight of this imposing, silent majesty, you may sense disbelief. Your initial shock of amazement wanes as you attempt to absorb all the splendor of the magnificent panorama before you. Perhaps the most superb canyon overlook of all is at the strategically placed Grand Canyon Lodge. From the patio or through picture windows of the lodge's Sun Room there is showtime drama from sunrise to sunset, when first or last fiery rays torch the tips of purple-shadowed canyon temples.

There are times when it seems that the sky has fallen. You can look down on a thunderstorm in the canyon or watch a heavy layer of fog flow over the rim in billowing, slow-motion cascades to shroud all but the crests of the most lofty sentinels. The real action comes when a nighttime storm takes temporary possession of the canyon. Jagged lightning splits the dark while thunder reverberates from walls, buttes, and temples.

Paved highways lead to three more canyon views: Cape Royal, Angels Window, and Point Imperial. Six trails wind through the forest or follow the rim. Try one, for there is no better place to meditate or to stretch both mind and vision than beside this vast sea of space, filled to the brim with noble beauty and total silence.

For reservations and information contact:
TW Services, P. O. Box 400, Cedar City, Utah 84720, 1-801-586-7686, TELEX 29-9714

forts constructed in Utah Territory was built at Pipe Spring to protect the ranch workers and their families.

According to tradition, the Pipe Spring name originated from an incident in which one of the original discoverers, William "Gunlock Bill" Hamblin, demonstrated his marksmanship by shooting the bottom out of the bowl of a smoking pipe. This picturesque, well-preserved historic Mormon fort served as a ranch house until 1923, when it was made a national monument in recognition of the early Mormon settlers' courage and foresight. Today a living history program recreates spinning, weaving, and baking arts for a firsthand view of pioneer life.

GRAND CANYON NATIONAL PARK: NORTH RIM

Returning to Fredonia, you head south on U.S. 89A toward the world-renowned Grand Canyon of Arizona, 73 miles away. The highway soon starts its climb of nearly 3,000 feet to Jacob Lake, a popular wayside stop for tourists who are hungry or needing a tank of gas.

From the Jacob Lake highway junction, Arizona State Highway 67 heads south through 44 miles of evergreen and aspen forests and wide mountain meadows to the North Rim of the Grand Canyon. You will not know that the Canyon is there until you get out of your car and take a few steps through the trees. Suddenly you are standing on the rim of an immense, deep, plunging chasm with towering sun-tinted rock forms—one of nature's greatest wonders. Truly you are on the brink of an awesome and majestic dimension of time, space, color, light, shadow, and silence.

As you look for the Colorado River a mile below, your line of sight transects four life zones: the Canadian, Transition, Upper Sonoran, and Lower Sonoran, each with its own varieties of plants and animals. Along with the 5,000-foot drop in altitude from rim to river, temperatures consistently vary about 30 degrees.

This incredible canyon, averaging nine miles in width, was scoured out of a mile-thick series of sedimentary rock layers by all the forces of nature's elements: heat, cold, ice, sand, roots, earth tremors, and gravity. For about 13 million years they have worked in close harmony with the abrasive, silt-laden Colorado River. Tributaries bring debris eroded from a 150,000-square-mile area. It is estimated that before construction of Glen Canyon Dam, in one day at high flood stage the Colorado carried over two and a half million tons of the rasping rock, sand, and silt that gouge the canyon walls along the way.

More than a dozen geologic layers are visible at the Grand Canyon. To the casual observer these colorful stratified formations are a work of art. But to the geologist they are much more. In biting deeply into the earth's crust, Time and the River have exposed the orderly pages of an illustrated

DAVID MUENCH

Bright Angel Point enjoys the grandest command performance of them all. Here the vast east-west canyon panorama is a natural stage for dramatizing the first and last rays of the sun. Daybreak lifts the curtain on the first red glow of the temple tips. Then canyon shadows submit to the overpowering glory of the rising sun. Cautiously they explore their precipitous descent a mile down as they hide in the Inner Gorge. Slowly they meander around to the afternoon side and climb back to the rim, silently clothing the canyon in deep purple mist in preparation for the mysterious blanket of night.

text. These pages narrate the story of the earth's creation, starting two billion years ago with some of the oldest rock on earth—the black schist exposed by the River's deepest cut. Each layer, with its telltale fossils and composition, illustrates the geologic stairway that life on earth climbed through the ages.

The Kaibab Plateau slopes southward; thus water from rain and snow deposited on the northern rim drains *into* the Canyon. On the South Rim much of the water flow is also southward, *away* from the Canyon. Therefore, the north wall recedes more sharply, leaving the river channel closer to the South Rim. An additional contribution to variation in canyonside erosion is the 25-inch average annual rainfall on the north side versus 16 inches for the south. If there are eight or ten feet of snow on the North Rim, it is likely that snowfall measures four or five feet on the South Rim and that there is none at all at the bottom of the Canyon.

The lone buttes and mesas in the sea of space between canyon walls have been gnawed free from ancient rim areas by eroding side canyons that eventually joined, isolating former portions of the Colorado Plateau.

Heavy stands of evergreen and quaking aspen rise past expansive flower-decked meadows all the way across the Kaibab Plateau right to the edge of the Grand Canyon's North Rim. Here they frame the colorful array of buttes, temples, and mesas thrusting up from the gorge far below. The ever-changing weather moods, the shift of lighting from dusk to dawn, and seasonal changes offer a never-the-same variety of views.

The crescendo—day's end at Monument Valley.

As you look across the Canyon you will see on the far side the forested South Rim, approximately 1,000 feet below you. By trail it is 14 miles from the North Rim to the Colorado River and 7.8 miles more to South Rim Village. It is less than 22 miles on foot or by mule, 9 miles by air, but more than 200 miles by car. Two additional North Rim viewpoints reached by park highways are Cape Royal and Point Imperial.

Six North Rim nature trails, averaging from a third of a mile to 12 miles in length, and the 14-mile Bright Angel Trail down to the River offer hikers a variety of workouts. If you have time, the best way to round out your Grand Canyon experience is to see it from the inside out by taking a muleback ride down the trail to Roaring Springs. This round trip can be completed in one day. Arrangements can be made at the lodge.

Meals and cabins are available at the North Rim's Grand Canyon Lodge. There is also a campground nearby. All are open from mid-May to mid-October.

After you have left the grandeur of the North Rim, you will drive back via Arizona Highway 67 to the Jacob Lake junction. From there U.S. 89A winds down from the forested Kaibab Plateau eastward onto the wide sweep of House Rock Valley. Seventeen miles east of Jacob Lake a dirt side road leads south about 22 miles to a vast buffalo range where a protected herd wanders with all the apparent freedom they enjoyed a hundred years ago.

Back on U.S. 89A, as you skirt the base of the lofty Vermilion Cliffs on your way northeast, you will spot a tiny oasis hugging the base of the cliffs. This is Cliff Dwellers Lodge. This little haven was developed by northern Arizona tourism pioneer Art Greene and his family, who at one time lived beneath the strange, naturally shaped toadstool formations in this area.

A few miles farther east at Marble Canyon, steel-girdered Navajo Bridge crosses the walled-in Colorado River, 467 feet below. The bridge is just seven miles downriver from historic Lee's Ferry. On the east side of the bridge the highway reenters the Navajo Reservation. Fourteen miles beyond the bridge, 89A joins U.S. 89, which, turning northward, ascends the Echo Cliffs. From their crest you can see the vast panorama of the valley you have just crossed. The Kaibab National Forest looms dark on the distant skyline. Below, the Colorado River cuts a ragged gash through Grand Canyon National Park. As U.S. 89 slices through a deep notch at the crest of this red escarpment, you are now on the home stretch. From here it is only 20 miles back to your starting point at Lake Powell's Wahweap Marina.

DICK DIETRICH

There are scores of additional things to see and do throughout this entire "linger-a-while" land— far too many to do justice to in the space allotted here. Each park, each monument, each place has its own personality . . . its own character . . . its

own individual charm. In seeking out the many historic and scenic landmarks, you will have the added
enjoyment and pleasure of personal discovery when
you take the Grand Circle Adventure.

For further reading: Bryce Canyon, Canyon de Chelly, Capitol Reef,
Glen Canyon–Lake Powell, Grand Canyon, Zion—all from "The Story
Behind the Scenery" series.

Order from: KC Publications • Box 14883 • Las Vegas, NV 89114
Printed by Dong-A Printing Co., Ltd. • Seoul, Korea